STRANGE & UNUSUAL
CREATURES

Beekman House

CONTENTS

Louis Weber, C.E.O.
Publications International, Ltd.
7373 N. Cicero Avenue
Lincolnwood, IL 60646

Permission is never granted for commercial purposes.

Manufactured in Yugoslavia
h g f e d c b a

ISBN: 0-517-02738-0

This edition published by Beekman House, Distributed by Crown
Publishers, Inc., 225 Park Avenue South, New York, New York 10003

Library of Congress Catalog Card Number: 90-60055

Written by: Geraldine Marshall Gutfreund
Picture credits:
Animals, Animals: 41, 98, 104, 124, 126; Roger and Donna Aitkenhead:
68; Kathie Atkinson: 7; M. Austerman: 42, 54; Anthony Bannister: 8; G. I.
Bernard: 96; M. A. Chappell: 38, 66; John Chellman: 43; E. R. Degginger:
30, 36, 84, 103; Michael Dick: 22; Michael Fogden: 6, 72; David Fritts: 28;
Johnny Johns: 12; Breck P. Kent: 88,120; Richard Kolar: 5, 67; Zig
Leszczynski: 14, 31, 35, 52, 83, 86, 92; C. C. Lockwood: 26, 123; Raymond
Mendez: 47, 107, 110, 114, 116; Stefan Meyers: 44, 56; Charles Palek: 10,
11; John L. Pontier: 108; Fred Prenzel: 60, 64; Maresa Pryor: 58; Auril
Ramase: 102; Ralph Reinhold: 87; Carl Roessler: 74, 75; George Roos:
115; Leonard Lee Rue III: 18, 23, 32, 34; Len Rue, Jr. : 50; C. W. Schwartz:
70; Donald Specker: 106, 112, 122; Marty Stouffer: 16, 20; Jim Tuten: 55;
Jack Wilburn: 39; Ernest Wilkinson: 48. **Bruce Coleman, Inc.:** 91; A.
Blank: 128; Rod Borland: 63; E. R. Degginger: 15, 82; Joe McDonald: 99;
C. D. Plage: 90; Hans Reinhard: 78, 79, 80; John Shaw: 100; Kim Taylor:
94, 95; John Uisser: 62; Peter Ward: 111. **Tom Stack & Associates:**
Dominique Braud: 59; W. Perry Conway: 27; David M. Dennis: 127; Jeff
Foott: 51; Gary Milburn: 19, 46; Joe McDonald: 71; Rod Planck: 36; Ed
Robinson: 76; John Shaw: 119; D. Wilder: 118.
Front Cover: Anthony Bannister/Animals, Animals; **Front Flap:**
Z. Leszczynski/Animals, Animals; **Back Cover: Animals, Animals:**
E. R. Degginger, Joe McDonald, Leonard Lee Rue III, Marty Stouffer;
Back Flap: Z. Leszczynski/Animals, Animals.

INTRODUCTION

It is easy to love a cute puppy. And it is easy to admire a majestic lion. It is even easy to willingly reach out to feed a peanut to a huge elephant. But other animals are not as easy to love. We shrink away from a bat. We think of snakes and frogs as slimy. And when we see a wolf, we think of poor Little Red Riding Hood.

Why have some strange and unusual animals become nature's unlovables?

Animals, such as snakes and spiders, are unlovable because we think of them as dangerous. But even animals that hurt us are not simply mean—they are usually just defending themselves. Animals, just as people, will defend themselves if they think someone is going to hurt them. In most cases, only a few species are actually harmful.

Wolves are unlovable because they prey on more lovable animals, such as deer and moose. But the deer actually need their predators. The predators kill the old and sick animals, which keeps the general population healthy. Without predators, there would be too many deer and too little food to go around. The population would begin to starve. It may seem cruel, but this is part of the natural order.

Some unusual animals, such as skunks, are unlovable because we think of them as dirty or smelly, and others are unlovable because they have become pests to us. Creatures such as moles, foxes, and cockroaches are acceptable to people—as long as they aren't making holes in their yards, eating their chickens, or running across their kitchen floors.

Scavengers, such as vultures, are unlovable because they eat things that are already dead. We think of these animals as disgusting. But without them, the world would be less pleasant. Some animals, such as warthogs, are unlovable because they seem just plain ugly to us.

All of these strange, unusual, and unlovable animals have something in common. They are misunderstood. If we learn something about these unlovable animals, we may find that they are not as dangerous as we thought, or at least we will understand why and when they are dangerous. We will discover reasons to admire them. We may find that they are not cruel, but are actually doing their job in the world. We may find that they are not dirty, disgusting, or really ugly, but interesting.

Let's meet what first appear to be nature's strange, unusual, and unlovable creatures. You will discover their place in the world that we all share together.

This crab spider gets ready to enjoy a cricket supper. Crab spiders are so named because they scuttle sideways as crabs do.

BATS

This tent bat has long arms and long, membrane-covered fingers that allow it to fly.

Bats! What do you think of when you think of bats? Do you think of a witch's stew, Halloween, a screech in the dark, something getting into your hair, or an evil chill in the air?

Perhaps because most species of bats are nocturnal (active at night), people associate them with evil. People are afraid of bats because they do not know much about them.

There are 951 known species of bats, and new species are still being discovered by scientists. Bats, like people, are mammals. They have backbones and hair, and they nurse their young with milk. They are also warm-blooded, meaning that their body temperature can be adjusted internally rather than being

dictated solely by their environment. Just as you have arms and legs, bats have front and back legs. They also have a skin membrane covering their arms and hands. They have a thumb, which is not covered by the membrane, and is used for moving around their roosts. The rest of their finger bones are basically the same as yours, although they have adapted to fit the way bats live. Bats are the only mammals that have wings that flap. Other mammals that are said to fly, such as flying squirrels, only glide.

Bats are found all over the world, except in the polar regions. They can live anywhere on land, except

These gray-headed flying foxes are just "hanging out" in a tree.
Most species of flying foxes navigate by sight.

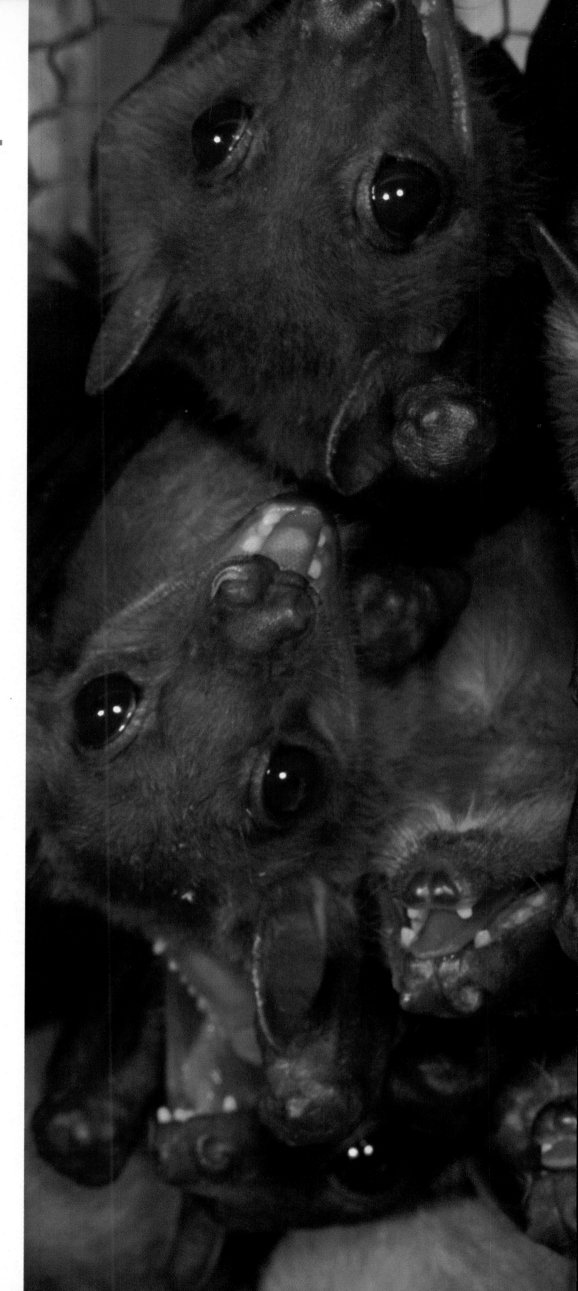

on the highest mountains. A group, or colony, of bats roosts in caves, holes (tree holes), and in the open, where they generally hang upside down from something such as a cave roof or tree branch.

Most bats eat insects. Different species also eat scorpions, mice, other bats, lizards, frogs, fish, fruit, flowers, pollen, nectar, and leaves. A few species feed on the blood of mammals or birds. The common vampire bat, found from Mexico to South America, feeds on the blood of domestic cattle. This is the bat that has given the other species of bats an undeserved bad name. The common vampire bat originally fed on wild animals. It turned to domestic animals because people brought their cattle to graze in areas where wild animals used to live. This bat is not being evil—it is surviving in the only way possible.

Nighttime is feeding time for these mammals. How do bats find their way to their food in the dark, even when that food is a tiny insect? They use *echolocation*. As you read this word, you will see that it is made up of two words that you know: "echo" and "location." Bats make squeaks too high for humans to hear. They are able to hear the echo of these squeaks as they bounce off of their prey and other objects. Because of this ability, bats find their food easily without bumping into things.

Bats are generally harmless creatures. Some species even serve an important function. Certain spear-nosed bats and bats known as flying foxes disperse seeds and pollinate plants. In North and South America, over 500 species of plants are pollinated by bats.

Many species of bats are endangered. Organizations, such as Bat Conservation International, are working to protect bats from extinction and to educate people about them. Bats are not evil creatures. They are just one of many types of animals in nature that we need.

These Egyptian fruit bats are roosting in a cave in South Africa. During the day, bats usually cluster together and rest in dark places, such as caves or church belfries. At night, they venture out to find food.

WOLVES

These playful gray-wolf pups can live for up to 20 years in captivity.

Who's afraid of the Big Bad Wolf? When you think of wolves, do you think of the wolf huffing and puffing at the doors of the three little pigs or of the wolf pretending to be grandma in Little Red Riding Hood? Maybe you think of the werewolves we see in horror movies or read about in books. Wolves have been cast as villains that prey on innocent animals and people. Let's find out the true story of wolves.

Wolves belong to the same family as domestic dogs and foxes, but are more closely related to dogs. Many scientists think that wolves are the ancestors of domestic dogs.

Today, there are two species of wolves. Gray wolves (also called timber wolves and white wolves) live in North America, Europe, Asia, and the Middle East. They can live in forests, tundra (frozen, arctic plains), deserts, plains, and mountains. These wolves can weigh up to 175 pounds. The World Wildlife Fund lists these wolves among animals that are in danger of extinction. Much of their habitat has been destroyed, and they have been actively hunted by people.

Red wolves are smaller, weighing up to 70 pounds, and were once found in the southeastern United States. They are now endangered and few exist in the wild.

These animals usually mate for life. They live in family groups or

Despite its name, the gray wolf may actually have black or white fur, depending on where it lives.

packs, sometimes with as many as 20 members. Usually, only one pair from the pack of wolves breeds, and they have a litter of four to seven pups in late spring. Wolves have been called the best parents in the animal world. Not only the parents, but the other wolves in the pack help raise the cubs. They are like aunts and uncles.

Wolves hunt large animals, such as moose, caribou, and deer, in packs. Usually, they kill only the old and sick animals, which keeps the rest of the herd healthy and ensures that there will not be too many animals for the available food supply. Farley Mowat, in his wonderful book, *Never Cry Wolf*, tells an Eskimo story in which the God of the Sky wants the wolves "'to eat the sick and the weak and the small caribou, so that the land will be left for the fast and good ones.'" Wolves also eat mice, beavers, rabbits, birds, fish, insects, and berries. There are very few cases of wolves attacking people.

Wolves are not bad. They are intelligent, family-loving animals that are only doing their job as predators to keep nature in balance.

Today, wolves, which have been persecuted by people for so long, need our help in providing refuges for their survival. One such refuge is the Alligator River National Refuge in North Carolina, where four pairs of red wolves have recently been released into the wild. Hopefully, these wolves will survive and breed so that people can finally appreciate their role in nature.

Wolves are highly intelligent creatures that live and hunt in packs. They communicate with each other using many sounds, such as whines, grunts, yips, barks, and, of course, the familiar howls.

SKUNKS

This striped skunk is busy digging for insect grubs. It is the most common species of skunks.

P.U.! Is that what you think when you hear the word "skunk"? Skunks are best known for the smelly fluid, called musk, that they squirt at their enemies. Musk comes from glands at the base of a skunk's tail and is used as a defensive weapon against predators. If the wind is right, skunks can squirt a distance of up to 23 feet, although they can only aim accurately for about 6 to 12 feet. A skunk's spray can cause severe nausea and temporary blindness, and its smell of rotten eggs lingers for days.

Skunks' black and white coloring is actually a warning to other animals that they should be left alone.

Most species of skunks further warn their enemies before they spray by stamping their feet and raising their tails. Spotted skunks actually do a handstand before spraying.

It is no wonder that skunks are best known for their smelly weapon! This weapon defends them well against their predators. The only animal that preys regularly on skunks is the great horned owl. But there is more to skunks than their smell. Let's find out about these creatures that are helpful to people —as long as we don't get too close.

Skunks are found in North, Central, and South America. They are

This charming trio of bushy baby skunks is exploring life in Al-
berta, Canada. Skunks prefer to live in open spaces.

related to weasels, otters, and badgers. The 13 species of skunks live in woods, plains, deserts, and even cities. They dig burrows or live in the abandoned burrows of other animals, such as foxes. In cities, they may live under buildings. Never get close to a wild skunk—not only do skunks spray, they are also a major carrier of rabies.

Most skunks are nocturnal (active at night). They forage at night for food. Skunks eat insects, small mammals, grubs, birds' eggs, and fruit.

Depending on the species, skunks give birth between April and May to between 2 and 9 young, called kits. Male and female skunks live apart except for mating, and the males leave all child-rearing to the females.

How do skunks help people? Skunks keep us from being overrun by mice—they eat even more mice than cats do. Skunks also eat many insects that destroy crops, such as crickets, cutworms, grasshoppers, potato beetles, June bugs, and grubs. Skunks may eat more insects than all other mammals combined. In New York, skunks ate so many of the grubs that were killing an important plant that people demanded full protection under the law for skunks.

Remember, leave skunks alone and they will leave you alone! But if you do get sprayed, naturalists say that washing in vinegar or tomato juice may help you remove the smell.

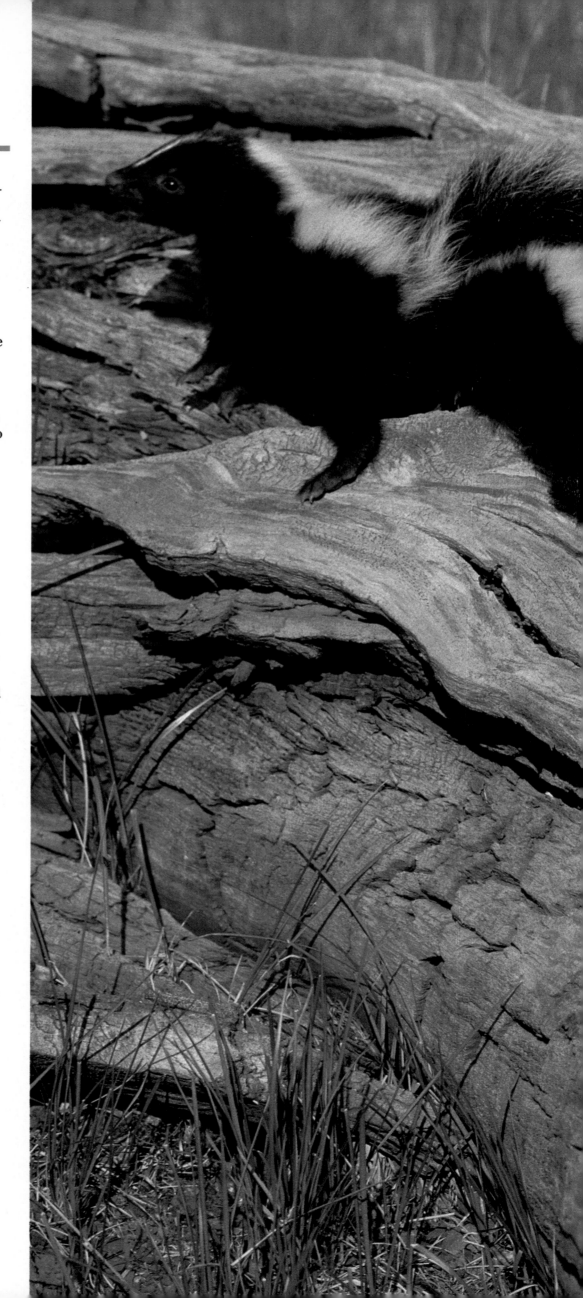

These baby skunks may be cute, but they are *wild* animals. They should not be taken from the wild and deodorized to be kept as pets. Indeed, in some states, keeping skunks as pets is illegal.

WOLVERINES

In winter, wolverines often prey on reindeer when the snow is soft.

Wolverines are members of the mustelid family, which is also called the weasel family. Skunks also belong to this animal group. Although they are perhaps not as looked-down-upon as their smaller cousins, skunks and weasels (called the "Dracula of animals"), wolverines have a bad name, too.

Another name for the wolverine is glutton (someone who overeats all of the time). An old story tells of a wolverine eating until its stomach is "tight as a drumstick," and then squeezing between two trees until its stomach is empty and it can eat some more. This is just a story, but what are the facts about the wolverine or glutton?

Wolverines, which weigh between 22 and 55 pounds, are the largest of the mustelid family. They are found in the arctic and subarctic regions of North America, Europe, and Asia. They live on plains called tundras and in fir forests called taigas. They have been known to tear apart cabins and destroy the contents in search of food. This has not made them popular with people who live in these areas!

In the winter, wolverines eat reindeer and caribou. In contrast to deer hooves, which sink easily in soft snow, wolverine hooves are large and broad and can handle soft snow well. So, even though deer can usually outrun wolverines in sum-

In the past, wolverine fur was considered so valuable that a Siberian city is said to have put a wolverine image on its coat of arms.

mer, wolverines can usually catch deer in winter.

Wolverines are good hunters, but they are also scavengers, eating the remains of animals killed by other predators. The deer or caribou carcass is often torn apart by wolverines and hidden in crevices or buried for later use. Perhaps this habit has given the wolverine its reputation of being a greedy glutton, even though these stores of food will stay good in their cold habitat and will be needed later. The mother wolverine will need these stores of meat to feed herself and her kits.

Female wolverines give birth to one to four young, called kits, between late January and early April. The kits and their mother will stay in or near the den, which the mother has dug for them, until early summer. They will stay near their mother until they are almost grown in the fall. Just like their skunk cousins, male wolverines do not take an interest in raising their young.

In summer, when food is more plentiful, wolverines eat birds, small mammals, and plants. They also scavenge the remains of deer calves killed by predators such as lynx, grizzly bears, and wolves.

Though not considered endangered animals, there are not as many wolverines as there were 100 years ago. Their habitat is being taken over by people and they are still being trapped for their fur. Some scientists feel that wolverines are vulnerable, meaning that they may be in danger of becoming extinct in the future.

A wolverine in Montana snarls for the camera. Wolverines, like their skunk relatives, have the ability to produce a foul-smelling liquid to help ward off would-be attackers.

WARTHOGS

This East African warthog is wallowing in a mud hole to keep cool and to protect itself from insects.

A face only a mother could love? Warthogs, with their gray skin, bristly hair and manes, thin tails, and long faces covered with warts (most pronounced in the males) are certainly candidates for the most ugly animal award. In addition to a smaller set of lower tusks, the males also have a large set of curving, upper tusks. These tusks usually grow to a length of about 1 foot, but have been known to grow over 2 feet long. Add to their appearance a fondness for mud baths, and warthogs will definitely win the ugly prize. But there is more to the warthog than meets the eye.

Warthogs are wild pigs. They are found in Africa and live in grassy and wooded plains called savannas. Warthogs weigh between 110 and 240 pounds, with the males being larger than the females. Warthogs eat mostly grasses. During the dry season, they root bulbs and other plants out of the ground with the tough upper edges of their noses.

These diurnal creatures (active during the day) forage for their food in family groups. While male warthogs, or boars, search for their food alone, female pigs, or sows, live in family groups with their piglets and other sows. These family groups are called sounders. There are usually two to four piglets born each year. They are born in an underground hole.

The male warthog's facial warts may help protect him against the
tusks of another boar during a fight.

Warthogs may not get the prize for beauty, but they are smart. Like their domestic pig cousins, warthogs wallow in mud to keep themselves cool and for protection from insects. In their book, *Inside the Animal World,* Maurice and Robert Burton tell the story of a mother warthog educating one of her piglets on the value of mud baths. The mother was seen with her three piglets in Africa's Infolosi Park. She and two of the piglets wallowed and were soon covered in mud, but one of the piglets stayed clean. The mother herded this piglet back to the wallow, got back into the mud herself, and rolled on her back. Finally, the third piglet joined its mother.

Why does the warthog have ugly warts? Scientists are not certain what these warts are used for, but they have theories. The pair of warts growing above the tusks (seen clearly in the male) may serve as an extra weapon in addition to the tusks. They may also help protect the warthog's eyes when it is grubbing for food. There could also be other possibilities of which scientists are not yet aware.

Animals, including warthogs, look and act the way they do because they have inherited traits from their ancestors that help them to survive in their environment. Warthogs may not win the prize for beauty, but how about a prize for interesting?

A mother warthog shows off her babies, called piglets. Female warthogs give birth to their piglets in underground holes. The piglets are weaned from their mother's milk at about three months of age.

GRIZZLY BEARS

These two grizzly bears have just caught themselves a salmon supper in Alaska's McNeil River.

Grizzly bears are the stuff that nightmares are made of! Weighing up to 975 pounds, they are one of the largest land animals. Grizzly bears can bite through a ½-inch steel bolt. We often picture them towering above us at their head to tail-tip length of 9.2 feet, their paws tipped with claws over 2 inches long.

It may come as a surprise that grizzlies eat mostly plants and that these bears have more to fear from people than the other way around. Indeed, American Indians believed that the grizzly was a great healer that breathed red, yellow, and blue dust from its nostrils while it healed them of sickness. So let's

find out more about the creature that early North American explorers Lewis and Clark knew as *Ursus horribilis,* or "horrible bear."

The term grizzly bear actually refers to three subspecies. Subspecies are animals of the same kind, or species, that have developed slight differences because they have been separated—usually by distance. The three subspecies are the grizzly bears, the Eurasian brown bears, and the Kodiak bears (although some scientists don't make a distinction between the grizzlies of North America and the Eurasian brown bears). The bears that live along the coasts and on the islands of Alaska are called Kodiak bears. Kodiak

Grizzly bears use their long, sharp claws to dig up roots. Today's grizzlies survive on a diet made up of leaves, roots, and berries.

bears, which are reported to weigh as much as 1700 pounds, are larger than the inland bears, that most people call grizzly bears. All three of these subspecies can be called grizzlies or brown bears.

Even though they are called brown bears, grizzlies can range in color from cream to cinnamon to black. Their fur is often white-tipped, which is where the name "grizzly" comes from—"grizzled" means sprinkled with gray. These bears have a dish-shaped face and distinctive shoulder hump.

Grizzlies live in woods. They are found in Europe, Asia, and North America. In North America, grizzlies are found mainly in Alaska and Canada. They are also found in the mountains of Wyoming, Idaho, Montana, and Washington.

Even though scientists classify all bears, including grizzly bears, as carnivores (meat-eaters), since their ancestors ate meat, only polar bears are primarily meat-eaters today. Grizzly bears are omnivores (animals that eat both plants and meat). Their main diet is made up of grass, leaves, roots, and berries. Their long claws are used mainly for digging up roots! Grizzlies also eat insects, small rodents, salmon, trout, deer, and animals that they find killed by other animals.

Do grizzly bears ever attack people? Grizzlies have attacked people, but usually the bear will simply leave if it sees a human in its path. Some scientists think that most attacks by bears on people are made because bears have bad eyesight and mistake humans for other bears that have invaded their range. The other cause of trouble between people and grizzlies is when bears learn to associate people with food. Bears rarely eat humans, but they are interested in picnic lunches. In parks where bears live, people are warned to keep food locked in their cars.

In many areas, grizzly bears are considered a threatened species. They are hunted out of fear and poached. Much of their habitat has been destroyed by mining and lumbering. Let's hope that people can learn to live with grizzlies.

A grizzly bear mother and her cub, like the pair from Arkansas shown here, will stay together until the cub is 1½ to 4½ years old.

FOXES

These red foxes usually have four to eight kits. Foxes breed once a year.

In the nursery story, "Henny-Penny," poor Henny-Penny, Cocky-Locky, Ducky-Daddles, and Goosey-Poosey are tricked by Foxy-Woxy into Foxy-Woxy's burrow. The familiar story tells us how the fox snaps off the other animals' heads. No wonder we think of foxes as tricky, bloodthirsty villains!

Are foxes really villains? Let's find out the facts.

Foxes are members of the same family as dogs and wolves. There are 21 species of foxes. They are found in all parts of the world, including both North and South America, Europe, Asia, Africa, and even Australia (where they are not native, but were introduced by Eu-

ropean settlers for fox hunts). Foxes live in a wide variety of habitats, including Arctic tundra, forests, prairies, deserts, and even cities. Foxes range in size from the small fennec fox, which weighs only about three pounds and lives in desert regions of northern Africa and the Middle East, to the small-eared dog fox, which weighs about 20 pounds and lives in tropical forests of South America.

The fox that most of us are familiar with and who is the Foxy-Woxy of our story is the red fox. Red foxes are not really typical of the other species of foxes. They are larger than most and live in a wide variety of habitats.

Some species of foxes are in danger of extinction. Fortunately, this bright-eyed red fox cub and its kind are not endangered.

Just like their cousins, dogs and wolves, foxes are carnivores (meat-eaters), but meat is not always their main diet. At the right time of year, 90 percent of a red fox's diet may be made up of blackberries, apples, plums, and grapes. Foxes are really true omnivores. They will eat anything! In addition to fruit, foxes eat mice, rabbits, birds, beetles, grasshoppers, and earthworms.

What has gotten the fox cast in the role of villain is its ability to seek food at farmstands and in cities. Foxes will scavenge in garbage cans, eat food set out for birds, and consume domestic animals, such as lambs and chickens. Red foxes, being nocturnal animals (active at night), can enter a hen house at night and kill every hen, carrying off just one chicken. This has led to the belief that the fox is a bloodthirsty murderer, killing chickens just for fun. Is this true? David MacDonald, a zoologist who has studied red foxes for many years, says in his book, *Running With the Fox*, "Does this prove that foxes are motivated by vicious bloodlust? The answer is no." Dr. MacDonald states that one possible explanation is a natural phenomenon found in other kinds of animals as well, in which an animal kills more than it needs. The fox uses its natural instincts to catch as many animals as possible. Foxes do this naturally with wild prey, burying the extra food for later use. A hen house full of chickens confuses a fox. It is possible that a fox's natural way of hunting is simply used with animals that cannot escape, leading to overkill. Whatever the explanation, the fox is not being deliberately mean. It is simply searching for food.

Naturalists also point out that foxes eat insects that might destroy crops and mice. Both of these activities are helpful to people.

So if you tell the tale of "Henny-Penny" to small children, don't forget to let them know that Foxy-Woxy has his good side, too.

Arctic foxes, also called blue foxes, live in northern polar areas. In winter, their coats are white or blue in color. In summer, their coats are gray-brown or chocolate-brown.

MOLES

A common mole pops out of its hole. Most species of moles are active both day and night.

You may have heard your mom or dad exclaim, "Oh, no! There's a mole in the yard!" You then noticed one or several mounds of dirt on your lawn. Although many people have seen molehills, moles themselves are seldom seen.

What is your mental picture of a mole? Do you think of an animal that looks like a blind mouse?

Moles are not totally blind. They cannot see sharply, but they do have complete eyes that are sensitive to light. Moles are not closely related to mice. They do not even belong to the rodent division of mammals as mice do. Moles belong to a group of mammals called insectivores. Scientists say that insecti-

vores are very primitive mammals with small brains. Unlike more advanced mammals, the brains of insectivores have few wrinkles, which decreases the surface area of their brains. They have primitive teeth and ears, too.

Although moles and other insectivores give us a clue as to what the earliest mammals were like, modern insectivores have evolved special features. It is one of these special features that gets moles into trouble with people. Moles have forelimbs that are permanently turned outward and are perfect for digging. Moles use these "hands" to dig permanent underground systems of tunnels. In most mole species, each

This hairy-tailed mole is on its way out of its hole. It is coming to
the surface to gather materials for its nest.

mole has its own territory, which it marks with a special scent that it secretes. Except for meeting briefly to mate or when a mother has her young, most species of moles live alone. They regularly dig a vertical shaft to the surface of the ground. This is a molehole. Moles do come to the surface, particularly to collect things with which to make nests for their young. One nest was found that was completely made out of potato chip bags. Most nests, however, are made of natural materials, such as grass.

As their classification as insectivores suggests, moles live on a diet of insects (such as beetles and fly larvae) and related creatures (such as earthworms). Moles will bite the heads off of earthworms (which does not kill an earthworm) and tie them in knots to store for future food. Moles are sometimes blamed for eating bulbs in gardens, even though they eat few plants. What they actually do is tunnel the ground, uprooting and killing young plants. This upsets people with gardens. But naturalists say that moles also destroy Japanese beetles, which feed on about 250 kinds of plants, including fruits, flowers, and vegetables.

So, if you hear someone complaining about moles, tell them that not only is the mole a fascinating creature living in a world of its own creation, it may also help save the roses.

Most male and female moles live apart; they get together only when it's time to mate. Male and female star-nosed moles, however, may actually live together in the winter. *Insert:* The star-nosed mole is named after the unusual pink tentacles that encircle its nose and serve as touch organs. This type of mole leaves its burrow often and is a strong swimmer.

RATS & MICE

The desert wood rat is a solitary rodent that is related to hamsters and gerbils.

At least among mammals, few animals are as unloved as rats and mice. It is not difficult to avoid certain mammals—like wolves and bears—but it is the rare home that has never had at least one mouse.

Because rats and mice are so common, most of us are familiar with at least a few species of the mouse family. This family contains 1082 species, including voles, lemmings, gerbils, and hamsters. They are found all over the world, with the exception of Antarctica. They live in all types of land habitats, except for snow-covered mountain peaks and in the high arctic, and are often the primary small mammals in their living area.

The animals that we commonly call rats and mice are really divided into two separate types, or subfamilies: New World rats and mice, which live in North and South America, and Old World rats and mice, which live in Europe, Asia, Africa, and Australia. There are 366 species of New World rats and mice and 468 species of Old World rats and mice. Certain New World and Old World species show similarities, but with so many kinds of rats and mice, there is much variation in how different rats and mice—even within the same subfamilies—live.

To illustrate this variety, let's look at a few species of New World rats and mice. The smallest member

This white-throated wood rat is scurrying into its home. Wood rats
collect sticks and bits of material to pile in their nests.

is the Pygmy mouse, which is so small that it weighs only one quarter of an ounce. It lives in grass nests, which are usually built under a stone or log. These mice eat seeds. In contrast, the largest member of the New World species is the South American giant water rat, which lives in moist areas and builds large burrow systems. One species of water rat can grow to an average length, from its head to the tip of its tail, of over 17 inches.

Some species of wood rats live in deserts. They often use pads of spiny cacti for material to make their homes. They also gather mounds of sticks to make their nests. Their habit of gathering and moving materials to their nest site gives them the common name of "pack rat." Other rats and mice live in forests, plains, fields, towns, cities, and maybe even in your house. Some types of rats and mice, such as Central American climbing rats, even live in trees.

Rats and mice eat mostly seeds, but different species also eat green plants, fruit, insects (one type of mouse is known as a grasshopper mouse), fish, snails, etc. In general, rats and mice have short life spans, but most members of the mouse family compensate by breeding early and often.

There can be no denying that rats and mice are destructive to food and clothing in homes and that they spread disease. We cannot forget, however, that they are food for a great many animals. Naturalists point out that they were even eaten by pioneers in emergency circumstances. Rats and mice have their place in nature, too.

The kangaroo rat hops about on its powerful hind legs. Although it is called a rat, the kangaroo rat is more closely related to the pocket mouse than to the more common brown and black rats found in urban areas.

LEOPARDS
(PANTHERS)

This curious black panther cub seems to have discovered its shadow.

Imagine that you are on the plains of Africa. Night is coming. You hear a rasping sound. You feel a shiver of fear, and you hide. There is a small antelope nearby. Suddenly, an animal drops from a tree. The antelope is killed and dragged up the tree ... You have just met the leopard.

Leopards, otherwise known as panthers, are found in Africa, the Middle East, and Asia. They live in tropical rain forests, plains, and mountains. There is only one spe-

cies of leopard. This species can be divided into seven subspecies, although all of these leopards are basically the same kind of animal. The seven subspecies are: the Amur leopard, the Anatolian leopard, the Barbary leopard, the North African leopard, the South African leopard, and the Zanzibar leopard.

Many people think that the black panther is a different kind of animal than the other leopards. What we call a black panther is simply a

The black panther is actually a leopard born with black fur, making
its black spots difficult to see.

leopard born with black fur. Leopards can also have coats of black spots on a cream-colored or light-brown background.

Leopards are members of the cat family. Their closest relatives are lions, tigers, jaguars, and snow leopards (snow leopards are a different species from what we commonly call leopards or panthers). Members of the cat family are all part of the group of mammals known as carnivores. Other carnivores are the dog family (wolves and foxes), the bear family, and the weasel family (skunks). Most carnivores eat a lot of things besides meat. Members of the cat family are true carnivores—they eat little besides meat.

Perhaps this is why leopards are so unlovable. Hunting mainly at night and alone, they seem to be animals whose main purpose is to kill. As with other predators, leopards are not killing for sport. They are killing for survival.

Many leopards have been killed for their fur. All subspecies of leopards, except for North African leopards, are endangered. Some scientists believe that the Zanzibar leopard may already be extinct. Leopards have few enemies, except for people. To a leopard, hunters must truly be unlovable!

Leopards drag their food into trees. An African story tells of how a leopard once shared its food with a jackal and hyena, but when they refused to return the favor, the leopard took to the trees with its food.

PORCUPINES

The prehensile-tailed porcupine spends much of its time perched in trees, where it snacks on leaves.

Would you hug a porcupine? Probably not. Would you gaze into the sky on a clear night and imagine that the stars of the Big Dipper are really the beautiful quills of porcupines? Again, probably not. Yet, according to an old Cheyenne Indian tale, the stars of the Big Dipper are a girl and her seven brothers who escaped from an angry buffalo into the sky. The stars twinkle because of the porcupine quills that were woven into their clothing.

To these and other North American Indians who lived with this creature, the porcupine, though not huggable, was an animal that was

appreciated. Porcupines were hunted for food; their quills were woven into clothing, boxes, necklaces, and bracelets.

Porcupines are rodents. There are two families of porcupines: New World porcupines and Old World porcupines. The 11 kinds of Old World porcupines live in deserts, open and rocky areas, and forests in Africa and Asia. They live on the ground and eat plants, roots, bulbs, and fruit. They also venture onto farms and eat crops, such as potatoes and pumpkins.

The 11 kinds of New World porcupines are found in Canada, most of the United States (including

This North American porcupine is enjoying one of its favorite foods—apples.

Alaska), Mexico, Central America, and much of South America. They can live in deserts, canyons, grasslands, and forests. They are generally arboreal (living mostly in trees) and eat tree bark, leaves, and fruit.

Most people think of porcupines as pests. Why? Porcupines love salt. Since a salt compound is often used to treat plywood, porcupines will chew through the wood to get to the salt. Salt is also used to make roads less slippery in the winter. When this salt collects on the undersides of cars and on tires, porcupines will chew on both to get to the salt. To the person who finds a chewed tire the next morning (porcupines are nocturnal and feed at night), porcupines are surely unlovable! North American porcupines feed on trees, which not only damages the trees, but also affects the lumber industry. In the modern world, are porcupines valuable? Let's find out.

You already know why North American porcupines are pests, but do these spiny animals also have their good points? One researcher found that porcupines are helpful in spreading apple seeds. Porcupines drop apple cores from trees. Deer mice eat these seeds and spread them, which, in time, produces more trees. Porcupines also eat only certain types of trees, enabling the active growth of others. Probably the porcupine's most useful function is its habit of eating the tops of trees. This encourages lower forest growth that, in turn, produces more food for such animals as white-tailed deer, snowshoe hares, moose, and songbirds.

Porcupines are a part of our world. Even if they do not have uses we are aware of, they are valuable simply as fellow creatures. Uldis Roze, who wrote *The North American Porcupine*, says that: "Time and again the porcupine has forced me to look at the forest, its natural home, in a different perspective. Again and again, the porcupine has been a teacher, a storyteller of the woods . . . adorner of the world."

This female porcupine is guarding her three-week-old baby. North American porcupines usually give birth to one baby after each mating. The mother will often hide its young in the base of a hollow tree to protect it.

KILLER WHALES

A killer whale's coloring helps it sneak up on its prey.

The very name—killer whale—is enough to get people shaking. This black and white whale can weigh almost 10,000 pounds and be over 30 feet long. It has a 6-foot long, triangular, sharklike fin on its back. There are about 44 strong, interlocking, cone-shaped teeth (10 to 14 teeth on each side of both jaws) in its mouth. Are you ready to run the other way from the animal that has been called the "wolf of the sea"?

These fearsome creatures are the same whales that you see at zoo shows. They are the same whales that deliberately avoid attacking man (there are no man-eating whales of any species), enjoy listen-ing to music, and play hide-and-seek with their trainers at the zoo.

Killer whales, like all whales, are mammals. Most scientists believe that the ancestors of whales were large land animals that lived along lagoons about 60 million years ago. Recent research suggests that the whale's closest living land-dwelling relative is the hippopotamus.

These mammals belong to a group of whales called the toothed whales. White whales, sperm whales, beaked whales, river dol-phins, dolphins, and porpoises are also toothed whales. The other group of whales are the baleen whales, which have no teeth. In-

From killer whales in captivity, scientists have learned how fast
they grow and how often babies nurse.

stead, they have plates of a material called baleen, which filters small creatures called krill out of the water for them to eat.

Killer whales, which are found in all of the oceans of the world, are the only whales that prey on other mammals. They eat dolphins, porpoises, other whales, seals, and sea lions. They also eat fish, squid, and seabirds.

It is the killer whale's hunting strategy that has earned it the reputation as the wolf of the sea. Like wolves, killer whales hunt in family groups. There can be between four and 40 whales in a pod, as these groups are called. There is usually one grown male for every three or four grown females. Both male and female young are in the pod—male calves may stay with their mothers for several years and female calves seem to stay with the pod for life. Killer whales can live for 50 to 100 years.

Killer whales have often been described as bloodthirsty killers. We must remember, however, that killer whales only hunt for survival. They kill only when hungry, and they usually kill only weaker animals.

It is easy to love killer whales when watching them in their close family groups. Killer whales are intelligent and loving. They communicate through a variety of sounds: clicks, squeals, and a high-pitched, singing sound. Mother whales have been seen reassuring their calves by "speaking" to them. In some ways, killer whales are not that different from people.

Like all whales, killer whales are mammals. Mammals breathe air through their lungs to survive. Instead of a nose, this whale has a blowhole, where its two nasal passages have joined into a single nostril.

VULTURES

The California condor is on the brink of extinction. All California condors now live in captivity.

An animal has died. A large, dark bird ready to feed is hovering in the sky. The bird, with a wingspan nearing 10 feet, begins to circle. Soon, more birds come. They swoop down with their bald-looking heads. They tear at the dead animal with their large, hooked beaks. Within twenty minutes, the dead animal is nothing but bones.

These birds are vultures. They are scavengers—they eat dead animals. Since we associate vultures with death, they seem frightening to us. They have even been credited with mysterious powers. African folklore says that vultures dream about dying animals so that they can find them and feed on them.

To the early Indian peoples of California, one vulture, the California condor, was a sacred bird. These people were right about vultures. Vultures are one of nature's most important animals. Think of what would happen to the bodies of dead animals if there were no vultures. Flesh would soon rot and provide a breeding ground for disease.

Vultures belong to a division of birds called raptors—birds of prey. Raptors include owls, eagles, kites, hawks, and falcons. Although most raptors eat carrion (dead flesh), many, including many types of vultures, do not kill to eat.

There are two families of vultures: Old World vultures and New

These vulture chicks are two weeks old. Parents take turns nesting with their young until they are able to find their own food.

World vultures. The fourteen species of Old World vultures are found in Europe, Asia, and Africa. New World vultures range from Canada to the tip of South America. The four species of New World vultures are the Andean condor, the King vulture, the Turkey vulture, and the California condor. Although both types behave in similar ways, there is one important difference—Old World vultures use only vision to find their food, whereas New World vultures use both sight and smell. Species in both families feed in groups.

The California condor is extremely endangered. Civilization is destroying its habitat. Condors have died from lead poisoning after eating animals shot by lead bullets; they have been shot by poachers; and they have been killed in collisions with power lines. Today, there are no California condors left in the wild. Scientists captured the six remaining birds in the wild and added them to captive populations in the San Diego and Los Angeles zoos in an attempt to build up the population. Baby condors have been bred from captive birds. The first baby California condor hatched in 1988; four more hatched in 1989. There are now 32 California condors. Scientists hope that they can soon return California condors to the wild, perhaps in the Grand Canyon area.

We need California condors and other vultures circling our skies to keep our world healthy.

Vultures often live together on cliffs or in trees. When breeding, a pair of vultures may nest apart from the others. Those that aren't breeding, however, usually roost and feed in groups.

ALLIGATORS & CROCODILES

Fish is the main staple of the alligator's diet, although it will eat larger animals.

Traveling through a swamp or river at night, you hear a bellow. You see the reddish glow of ancient eyes. In the water is the American alligator, an animal that can grow over 12 feet long. It is a member of the crocodilians, a group of reptiles that includes alligators and crocodiles.

Reptiles are animals that have scales, breathe air, usually lay shelled eggs, and are cold-blooded. Cold-blooded means that, unlike mammals and birds, reptiles cannot adjust their body temperature internally—they are dependent on outside temperatures. They are so different from mammals that people fear them. Fear of alligators and crocodiles has even given rise to stories of fire-breathing dragons!

The earliest crocodilians evolved about 200 million years ago. They all belong to a group of reptiles, called archosaurs ("ruling reptiles"), that once included dinosaurs. Although dinosaurs died out about 65 million years ago, crocodilians still share our world with us. Fossils of early crocodilians— dating back over 140 million years— have been discoverd, and these remains show few differences from the crocodilians living today. Scientists say that if these extinct species could be brought back to life and put in a zoo next to living species, many herpetologists (zoologists who study reptiles) would have a hard time telling them apart. Today, crocodilians include alliga-

Adult crocodiles and alligators, such as the American alligator
shown here, have few predators.

tors and the closely related caimans, crocodiles, the Tomistoma or false gharial, and, in a separate family, the gharial, a crocodilian from India. They inhabit swamps, lakes, rivers, and even coastal waters in warm climates. They can be found in North, Central, and South America; Africa; Asia; and Australia.

There have been changes in crocodilians in the last 200 million years. Through the ages, many varieties have existed, including those with duckbills, tall snouts, horns, and hooves. However, the basic crocodilian form that we see today in alligators and crocodiles has been the most successful in terms of survival and therefore has remained to this day.

One reason crocodilians have survived is their eating habits. Their food sources differ from those of mammals, so they have not had to compete with mammals for food. They can also survive on less food than mammals and can even slow down their growth when there is little food available in order to ensure survival.

Crocodilians today are in danger of extinction. Their habitat is being damaged and they are being hunted for their skins, which are used to make leather products, such as shoes and purses. The World Wildlife Fund lists 20 kinds of crocodilians as being in danger of extinction.

These reptiles can be useful in nature. For example, alligators in wetlands dig holes that can bring up the water that many animals depend on during a drought. Scientists also believe that crocodilians can provide clues to the early behavior of mammals and birds, whose ancestors were reptiles.

Crocodilians are the last of the ruling reptiles. They can arouse our fear, but they should also inspire our respect and imagination.

This saltwater crocodile in Australia is floating near the water's surface, waiting for unsuspecting prey. Crocodiles swim and feed in water, but they come onto land to lie in the sun and to breed.

SNAKES

This African egg-eating snake is spreading its jaws wide to swallow a large egg. The collapsed shell will then be regurgitated.

Slithery. Scaly. Ugly. Slimy. Is that what you think of when you think of snakes?

Snakes are reptiles. Scales are part of their skin and help keep them from getting too dry. They also protect them and help them move. A snake's skin is not slimy. It has a smooth, pleasant feel. If you are allowed to stroke a snake at a zoo or nature center, stroke it down in the direction of the scales. Stroking the scales in the opposite direction can hurt the snake.

Ugly? Many snakes are beautiful. Different snake species have a wide variety of markings and colors. Since snakes live in a variety of habitats, including deserts, forests

(mostly tropical forests), rivers, lakes, and even the sea, there is a wide variety of colorations and patterns. Most have colors that help them to hide from predators. Many snakes that live on the ground, for example, are brown or gray. Snakes that live in trees are often green; those in the desert may be yellow or red. Snakes that live in water may be light-colored on their undersides to blend in with light filtering through the water; this makes them less visible to predators below. These same snakes may be dark on their topsides to blend in with the dark water on the surface. Some snakes are brightly colored to serve as a warning to predators, and oth-

The sidewinder snake moves on unstable surfaces by raising its
head and thrusting it forward at a 45° angle.

ers with vivid colorations are harmless. They only look dangerous in order to fool predators. Whatever the reason for its coloring, a snake such as the rainbow boa, with its shimmering blue, green, and lavender scales could never be called ugly.

Snakes evolved about 120 million years ago. They are the reptile group that has evolved most recently and are found over most of the world. There are 2700 species of snakes. They range in size from the reticulated python of Southeast Asia, which can be up to 32 feet long, and the South American anaconda, which can be up to 30 feet long and weigh 330 pounds, to the tiny thread snakes of the West Indies.

All snakes eat meat. Most snakes have poorly developed senses of hearing and sight, so they depend on smell to locate their prey. The snake's forked tongue picks up scents that are then relayed to openings in the roof of its mouth. These openings lead to a special scent organ. Some species of snakes grasp small live prey, such as insects, fish, and tadpoles, in their mouths and swallow them. Others first kill their prey by coiling around the animal and suffocating it. Still other species poison their prey with venom before eating it.

Of the 2700 species of snakes, the venom of about 200 types is dangerous to people. In the United States, rattlesnakes, copperheads, water moccasins, and coral snakes are poisonous. Naturalists advise you to leave snakes alone and they will leave you alone.

Many snakes are helpful. For example, the banded water snake, which is often confused with a water moccasin, is harmless and helps keep water clean by eating dead fish. So don't judge all snakes by the dangerous few.

This poisonous Australian taipan snake can reach a length of ten feet. The taipan shown here is molting—sloughing off the outer layer of its skin. Snakes molt when they outgrow their skin, usually every two months.

IGUANAS

This banded iguana lives in captivity in the Fiji Islands. Iguanas are legally protected in many countries.

You are walking along a riverbank in South America. Suddenly, you look up into the trees. Above you is a group of 6-foot long, dragonlike lizards. They are awake, staring at you with cold, reptilian eyes. Iguanas! They leap 50 feet below. Are they after you? No. The iguanas jumped into the river and are swimming away from you because they fear people. In fact, iguanas feed almost entirely on plants. They will sometimes eat insects, chopped meat, and canned dog food in captivity, but their main diet is made up of fruit, flowers, buds, and leaves.

There are 30 species of true iguanas. They are members of the lizard division of reptiles. Iguanas are found in the southwestern United States, Mexico, Central and South America, Fiji, the Galapagos and Bahama islands, and islands in the Gulf of California.

Most iguanas live in dry areas, but some live in tropical forests or along the edges of forests. Iguanas live in holes, trees, among rocks, or in burrows. They lay their eggs in burrows in the ground.

Iguanas live between 10 and 40 years. On islands, where there were no mammals to compete with, they often grew larger and became the controlling animals. Today, many species of iguanas are in danger of extinction.

This marine iguana lives in the Galapagos Islands. Iguanas may
live between 10 and 40 years.

Destruction of their habitats is the main reason that iguanas are in danger: Dams have flooded the sandbars on which some iguanas breed, forests where others live have been cut down, and tourist development has destroyed other iguana homes. Iguanas are also in danger because domestic animals, such as pigs and goats, have been brought to islands where they did not live before. These animals compete with iguanas for food. Other animals, such as cats and dogs, which have also been brought to the islands by people, eat iguanas. People capture iguanas for food. They also take iguana eggs. Certain kinds of iguanas are captured to be sold as pets, which are often treated cruelly.

Iguanas and their habitats need protection. People must be educated that these giant lizards are not monsters, but timid plant eaters.

Schoolchildren in the Fiji Islands are helping to save the banded iguana. After they learned that the banded iguana is harmless, the children have made an effort to keep adults from killing them. Let's hope that banded iguanas and other iguana species can be saved.

These two dragonlike creatures are green iguanas. In some species of iguanas, the tail may be twice as long as the body. The iguana uses its tail for swimming and for defending itself.

FROGS & TOADS

This Cuban tree frog is one of the nearly 3,500 species of frogs and toads. About 630 of these species are tree frogs, which can be found in most tropical and subtropical areas of the world.

"Kiss me," says the frog, "and I will turn into a handsome prince." What would your answer be? Yuck? "Hug me, please," says the toad. You might say, "Ugh. I'll get warts!" What are frogs and toads like?

Frogs and toads belong to a group of animals called amphibians. Amphibians were the first group of vertebrates (animals with backbones) that could live, at least some of the time, on land. They evolved from a type of fish. Amphibians generally breathe air, are cold-blooded, have skin that must be kept moist, and return to the water to lay their eggs.

The ancestors of frogs and toads are fish. Baby frogs and toads—

tadpoles—look like their ancestors. Tadpoles hatch from eggs that are often laid in water. They breathe through gills just as fish do. However, not all frogs and toads lay their eggs directly in water. Some, such as many tree frogs, lay them on a leaf overhanging the water. After the eggs hatch, the tadpoles drop into the water. Other frogs carry as many as 100 eggs on their backs until they hatch. Then, they put the tadpoles in water or carry them until they are fully developed frogs. Some species even give birth to live young.

Even scientists sometimes call frogs toads and toads frogs. Originally, the name "frog" was given to

This wart-covered American toad has captured an earthworm for dinner. All adult frogs eat meat.

a species that was moist and slimy and jumped with long, back legs; the name "toad" was given to a species that was dry and warty and walked with short, back legs. This is just a general guide. For example, an animal called the midwife toad and an animal called the painted frog actually belong to the same biological family.

Frogs and toads are found in lakes, swamps, marshes, rivers, forests, grasslands, mountains, and deserts. Species that live in dry areas often survive by burrowing. Sometimes, they form a case of several layers of sloughed-off skin, which surrounds them and keeps them moist. When the wet seasons come, these frogs break loose from their cases and eat them.

Most frogs have a brown or gray coloring that helps them blend in with their surroundings. Some are brightly colored. Central and South American poison dart frogs are brightly colored and marked to advertise their powerful poison. This poison is used by native Indians to make poison hunting darts. Another brightly colored frog is the tomato frog from Madagascar. It looks just like a plump, ripe tomato!

Can you get warts from toads? No. People may have gotten this idea because many frogs and toads secrete either a poisonous substance or one that tastes bad as protection. This substance may irritate and burn the hands of people who pick them up.

Frogs and toads help people. They eat many insects, such as cutworms, which are harmful to crops, and gypsy moths, which are harmful to trees that give us shade and fruit. Naturalists estimate that these amphibians eat about 10,000 insects in three months.

Don't expect a frog to turn into a prince and don't hug a toad, but do take the chance to listen to your local frogs and toads. They were the first animals to develop a real voice and they may surprise you with how interesting and beautiful they really are.

This beautiful, but deadly, poison dart frog shows off its brilliant colors while transporting two tadpoles on its back. Some frogs blend in with their backgrounds; others change their colors to match their surroundings.

SHARKS

The wobbegong shark is a flattened shark that lives on the bottom of the sea and eats small fish and other sea animals.

Jaws? The horror of the deep? Man-eaters? Is that what you think of when you think of sharks?

Sharks have existed for about 400 million years. They belong to the fish group of animals, but, unlike most fish, sharks have few bones. Most of their skeleton is made of cartilage, the same substance that your ears are made of. Sharks live in all of the oceans of the world and some have been found in freshwater lakes and rivers.

Just because sharks were around before dinosaurs does not mean that modern sharks are primitive creatures. Scientists now know that sharks are highly specialized ani-

mals. Most species of sharks have large brains and highly specialized teeth. Each different species has just the kind of teeth it needs for the kind of food it eats. What's more, all sharks have several sets of teeth (they can have five or more sets of teeth at the same time). Why? Because sharks' teeth break often. So when a tooth breaks, a new one is ready to take its place. Some species of sharks actually lose whole sets of teeth at once.

Sharks have good vision and are more sensitive to light than people are. Sharks can smell so well that they have often been called swimming noses. Sharks are also able to hear low frequency sounds from

The great white shark is the most feared of the more than 350
types of sharks.

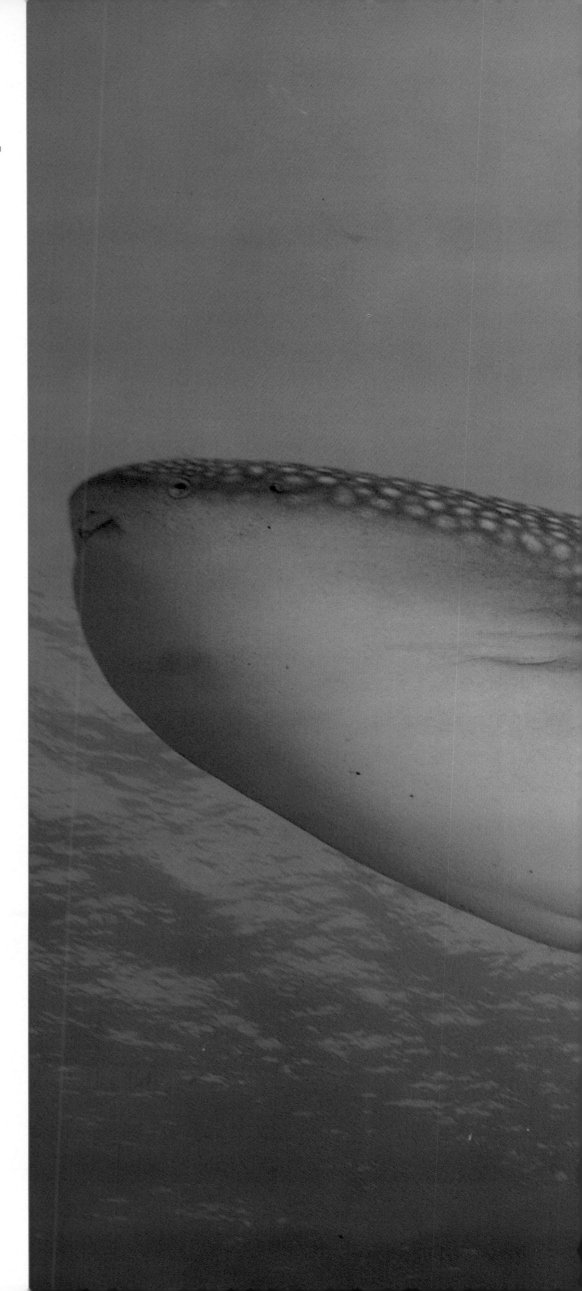

very far away. They have a special system that helps them detect vibrations in the water.

These creatures even have an extra sense. Sharks have special pores on their heads that can detect the weak electric field surrounding all animals, even people. These detectors help them find their prey.

Are sharks hunting for people? Not usually. There are about 350 known species of sharks. Of these known species, very few are dangerous to people. The chances of drowning are more than 1000 times greater than being killed by a shark. Of course, sharks have attacked people who ventured into their world, but most sharks don't seem to like human flesh. They often decide after the first bite of a person to let go. By then, it is too late. Shock and loss of blood may have already killed the person.

Even species of sharks that attack people, such as great white sharks and tiger sharks, may have mistaken them for their usual prey of seals and sea lions. Scientists point out that divers in wet suits look a lot like seals.

The largest species of sharks, whale sharks, can weigh up to 88,200 pounds and grow up to 59 feet in length. These giant sharks feed mainly on plankton—tiny sea plants and animals—that they strain from the water. They are so gentle that divers have held onto them for a free ride for miles.

With only a few species dangerous to people, sharks have more to fear from people than the other way around. Many sharks are killed for meat, leather products, and oil from their livers, as well as out of fear. Federal fishery managers think that some species may soon become extinct. Fortunately, scientists are learning more about these ancient creatures and letting people know that even sharks can be lovable.

Whale sharks are found in most tropical waters. This gentle whale shark was found swimming off the coast of Hawaii. Whale shark babies, called pups, hatch from the world's largest eggs (1 foot in length).

ELECTRIC EELS

Electric eels can produce a shock of nearly 600 volts—enough to stun a person or to kill fish and frogs.

An electric eel can discharge close to 600 volts of electricity. That is enough electricity to light up a neon light bulb. It is also enough to stun a horse . . . or a person. Repeated shocks could mean death.

Electric eels and true eels are both fish, but they are no more closely related. Electric eels look a little bit like true eels, but they are more closely related to carp.

The fish that we commonly call the electric eel is found in the Amazon River and its tributaries in South America. It is about 6 feet long. Electric eels are not the only fish that release electricity. They are part of a biological family of fish called gymnotids, which are

sometimes called electric gymnotids. Probably all of these gymnotids produce some electricity. Other kinds of fish besides gymnotids also produce electricity. Among these are stargazers, electric catfish, and electric rays. How do these fish produce electricity and what do they use it for?

In all animals, each time a muscle is contracted (tightened), a little bit of electricity is discharged. Electrical impulses in our nerves trigger an electric charge that spreads over the muscle, causing it to work. In people and other animals, this electricity is very weak. Special machines would be needed to detect the electricity being released. In

Adult electric eels have orange throats and long, olive-brown bodies that taper to pointed tails.

contrast, fish, such as electric eels, contain muscles fibers called electroplates that are so specialized that they do not tighten. They only generate electricity. Each electroplate produces only $\frac{1}{10}$ of a volt, but an electric eel has about six thousand of these special muscles in its tail.

Electric eels use electricity to kill their prey—fish and frogs. They can also use it to protect themselves. These charges even help them navigate to find their prey. Some scientists think that electric eels and other electric fish use their electric volts to communicate with each other. Whereas other animals might use sight, special scents, or certain actions to establish the leader of a group, to attract a mate, or to establish territory, these electric fish might do this by communicating with electricity.

What at first makes these fish frightening and threatening might open up a whole new world of study in the ways that animals communicate.

Most of what looks like the electric eel's body is actually its tail. Its internal organs are in a small space behind its head. The tail contains the organs that produce electricity.

SCORPIONS

These baby scorpions are getting a free ride on their mother's back.

Watching a shiny, black scorpion, a zoo visitor is surprised to learn that this fearsome creature bears live young, which it carries on its back until they molt for the first time and are able to survive on their own. (Molting refers to the scorpion's shedding of its hard skin, or skeleton, for a new skin. Scorpions molt seven or eight times in their lives.) The visitor didn't expect the scorpion to be such "a good mother." But the scorpion's maternal instinct serves much the same purpose as the scorpion's unlovable sting—it's part of nature's way of ensuring that scorpions survive.

Scorpions are invertebrates, meaning they have no backbone. Along with such animals as insects and spiders, they belong to the group of invertebrates called arthropods. *Arthropod* comes from the Greek words for "joint" and

This shiny, black scorpion is resting on a sea grape leaf in the Florida Keys. If left alone, most species will not harm people.

"foot." They have paired, segmented legs. Spiders and scorpions both belong to a division of the arthropod group called the arachnids.

Scorpions have four pairs of segmented legs. In front of these legs, which are for walking, they have armlike appendages with lobsterlike claws. The first thing that people usually notice about a scorpion, however, is its stinger.

The stinger is the last part of the scorpion's abdomen. With it, the scorpion can inject venom into its prey to defend itself or to control its struggling dinner. When used, the stinger arches above the scorpion to allow it to strike quickly. The venom can be as powerful as a cobra's in some species, or little more dangerous than a bee sting in others. Few species have venom powerful enough to seriously harm people. Scorpions first grab their prey with their claws. They tear the victim apart or crush it. Scorpions primarily eat spiders, other scorpions, and insects.

Scorpions would really rather run away and hide than sting a person. They hide by day under rocks, bark, or in burrows in the ground. They hunt at night.

The greatest danger to people is from scorpions moving into houses and hiding under beds, furniture, carpets, and even inside shoes! People in areas where scorpions live are often told to shake out their shoes in the morning before putting them on!

Scorpions are found in warm areas all over the world, especially in deserts. They range in length from ¼ inch to 8 inches.

Be careful if you live in areas where scorpions are found. If you do uncover one, leave it alone. Remember that a scorpion will only sting a person in self-defense. All animals have a job in nature—to ensure the survival of their kind. By protecting itself, the scorpion is doing its job.

This scorpion is getting ready to make a meal of a roach. Before attacking, some species of scorpions "sing" by rubbing the bases of their clawed "arms" against their first pair of legs.

SPIDERS

This female house spider has found a dark closet in which to raise her young.

In E.B. White's book, *Charlotte's Web,* Wilbur the Pig is horrified when his new spider friend, Charlotte, says that she eats insects; "'... Of course, I don't actually eat them. I just drink them—drink their blood. I love blood,' ... and her pleasant, thin voice grew even thinner and more pleasant." Poor Wilbur! But as Wilbur learns, a spider can be our best friend.

There are about 30,000 known species of spiders with new species still being discovered. Spiders are found all over the world in all types of land habitats. One type of spider even lives in the water.

Spiders are not insects. One easy way to determine this is to count their legs. Insects have six legs; spiders have eight. Insects have three body divisions; spiders have two. Most spiders have eight eyes, although some species only have six. Like their cousins, the scorpions, spiders also have an extra pair of armlike appendages in front of their four pairs of walking legs. And, as Charlotte told Wilbur, spiders drink the insides of their prey (not only their blood), instead of swallowing them whole. After capturing its prey, the spider pierces it with its fangs and releases poison into the victim. The spider then releases chemicals to turn the insides of its victim into liquid that it can suck up with its small mouth.

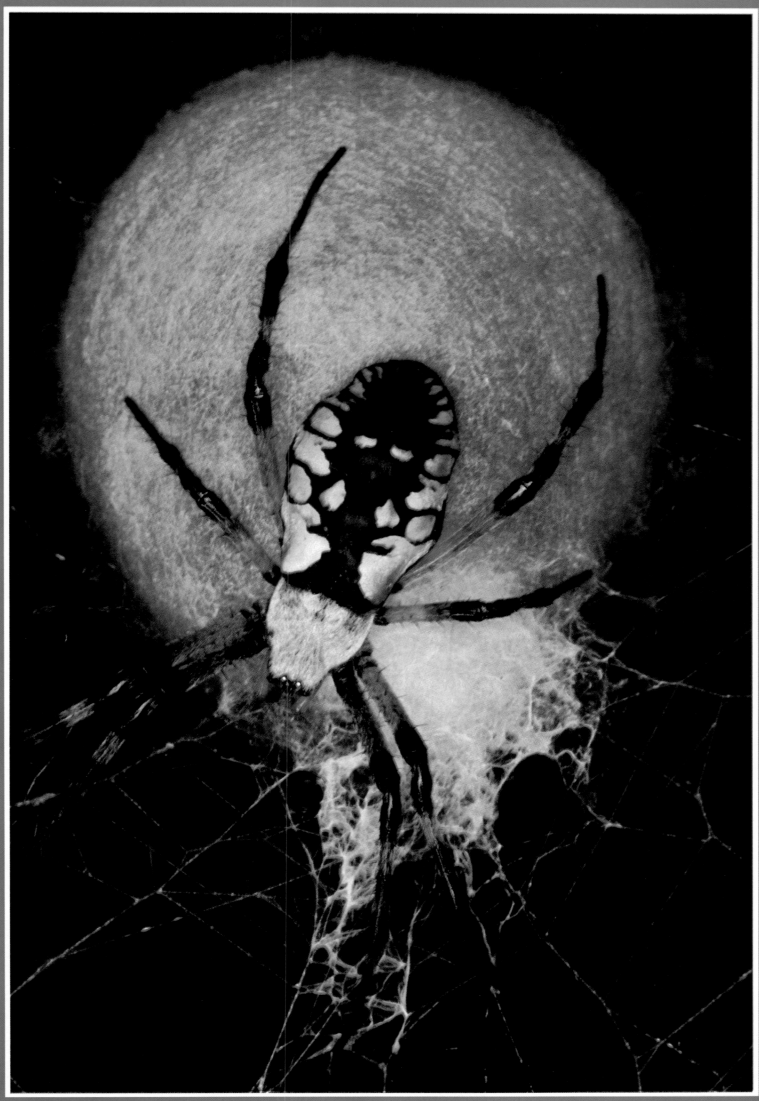

This black-and-yellow orb web spider weaves orb-shaped (circular) webs.

At first, it sounds as though Wilbur was right to be horrified with Charlotte's eating habits. But spiders are the best insect controllers we have. They eat silverfish, roaches, flies, mosquitoes, clothes moths, other insects, other spiders, and other arthropods. Some very large spiders, such as South American tarantulas, even eat birds. Very few spiders have venom that is dangerous to people. Those spiders that are dangerous to people, such as black widow spiders and brown recluse spiders, will not bite without being provoked. Nevertheless, you should be careful of them.

At the back of their abdomen (the second part of their body), spiders usually have three pairs of spinnerets. These are the organs that let spiders spin their silk for making webs, wrapping up their victims, and making egg-sacs for their eggs. Spinnerets also make a fluid that is used to make certain web strands sticky enough to catch prey. All spiders spin silk, but not all spiders make webs to catch their prey.

Some spiders catch their prey with trapdoors. These trapdoor spiders build silk burrows in the earth complete with a door. Insects coming close become dinner! Some species even spin strands of silk out from the doors to trip insects. Others ambush their victims. Spiders, such as crab spiders, can blend in with their surroundings and wait on a flower or leaf of the same color. They wait with their two pairs of front legs held out, enfold, and bite the insect that flies or crawls onto the flower. Other spiders, such as wolf spiders, stalk their victims and pounce on them.

Many species build webs. Besides the commonly seen round or orb web, some spiders build triangular webs; some build web nets to throw over their victims; and others, called bolas or angler spiders, spin a silk "fishing line" baited with a sticky gum that they cast at flying insects.

Spiders are fun to watch. Take it from Wilbur—a spider can be a true friend.

Light reflects off this beautiful, but dangerous, black widow spider. Only the female black widow has a poisonous bite. The female also has a red mark, often in an hourglass shape, on its underside.

CENTIPEDES

Notice how this speedy centipede's legs are bunched together on one side as it races across a log.

It's true
your name means hundred-legged
and I just have two,
but when I see you near my bath
you run one way, I run the other
and we both go very fast!

This rhyme describes how most people feel about centipedes—and how most centipedes feel about people! Centipedes, along with such insects as scorpions and spiders, are arthropods, but they are not insects. They have too many legs to be insects.

Do centipedes really have one hundred legs? Among the over 3500 species of centipedes, there are many differences. Some centipedes have as few as 15 pairs of legs—30 legs in all. Other kinds have as many as 177 pairs—354 legs in all. And if a centipede loses a leg, it grows a new one at its next molt.

How are centipedes able to walk and run on so many legs without tripping? Scientists have found that most centipedes move by alternately bunching together the legs on one side of their bodies and spreading the legs on the other side. A house centipede has been clocked clipping along at a speed of over 16 inches per second.

Centipedes need moisture to live. If left in uncovered, dry earth, a

A female centipede protects her eggs by curling around them.
The eggs are nearly bursting with yolk.

centipede will die in a few hours. This is why house centipedes are most often found in damp places, such as basements and bathrooms. They live in the soil, under bark and stones, in decomposing leaves, and in compost piles. There is even a type of centipede that lives on the seashore—in moist places under stones that are covered with water when the tide is high. Many types of centipedes are only 1 to 2 inches long, but some South American species can grow to be 1 foot long.

These creatures hunt for their prey at night when the air is moist. Centipedes find their way with a pair of sensitive antennas, since they have very poor eyesight. They mostly eat snails, slugs, earthworms, spiders, and insects. Large centipedes eat lizards and can even eat small snakes, birds, and mice. Centipedes kill their prey with a pair of poison claws, which are specialized hollow front legs connected to poison glands.

Few people have been killed by centipedes, although the bite of large, tropical centipedes can be dangerous. Even small centipedes should be avoided—their bite can hurt a lot.

House centipedes are helpful to people because they feed on silverfish, flies, and cockroaches. If you find a centipede near your bathtub—don't swat it. Watch it from a distance. Maybe it will set a new record for centipede speed!

This giant centipede has just shed its skin. Centipedes, as well as scorpions, spiders, and other arthropods, have an external skeleton and must molt as they grow.

FLEAS

Most species of fleas, such as these dog fleas, live away from their hosts much of the time.

A fox backs into a stream with a big piece of moss in its mouth. It backs into the water slowly until its tail is covered. Little insects begin jumping from the fox's tail onto its back. The fox goes further into the water. The insects jump further up the fox's back, toward the piece of moss and *away* from the water. Soon, the fox is submerged and all the insects are on the piece of moss. The fox lets go of the piece of moss. Its nagging parasites—fleas—float away.

Scientists are not sure if foxes really do rid themselves of fleas in this way, although many reports claim that they do. Many mammals and birds try almost anything to get rid of these pests.

There are 1600 species of fleas. Different species live on different kinds of animals. There are dog fleas, cat fleas, rat fleas, rabbit fleas, poultry fleas, mole fleas, etc. There are even fleas that live on humans! Some types of fleas, such as rabbit fleas, feed only on one specific kind of animal. Other fleas are not as choosy and may take a bite from any handy mammal or bird. More than 40 flea species will feed on people!

Throughout time, people have battled fleas. A recipe over 3000 years old suggests that date flour and water be boiled and then vomited in order to get rid of fleas. In the 1700s, people, especially

This bird flea is clinging to the feather of its host. One species of
bird flea has been found in the nest of an Antarctic bird!

women, wore flea traps—little cylinders with small holes that surrounded a rod covered with blood or honey to attract fleas—around their necks. Some of these flea traps even came with a little microscope so the wearer could study the fleas!

Fleas are insects. Insects have three body parts, three pairs of legs (six in all), and usually have two pairs of wings in their adult form. Fleas, however, do not have wings. Most scientists think that the ancestors of the flea had wings, but that modern fleas lost them and developed powerful jumping legs to help them reach their hosts. Wings would only be in the way once a flea jumped on its furry host.

These unlovables are parasites—they live off of another animal (called the host) by feeding off of it. The host animal is generally not killed by the parasite, since it would be of no advantage to the parasite. It would only lose its breakfast, lunch, and dinner. Fleas suck the blood of their hosts. They have special mouth parts that allow them to do this, as well as a special chemical in their saliva that they inject into the host to keep its blood from clotting.

People have good reason to find fleas unlovable. Through their saliva, they spread the germs of a sick host to the next host. Many animals can become infected this way. During the Middle Ages, a terrible disease called the bubonic plague was spread from rats to people by rat fleas. Since doctors did not know about antibiotics in the Middle Ages, this disease killed one quarter of all the people in Europe in five years (1347-1352). It was called the Black Death. Fleas can also spread another disease called typhus.

The only people who have found fleas lovable were the people who ran flea circuses. They made tiny carriages for them to pull, tightropes for them to walk on, and even little tricycles for them to perform on. Flea owners may have fed their fleas on their own arms, but to most people—fleas are no fun!

Some fleas feed on only one type of host. This rabbit flea, for example, has found itself a rabbit's ear. Fleas have been around for a long time. A flea fossil dating back 50 million years has been found.

MOSQUITOES

Of the 100 species of mosquitoes that can carry malaria, about 60 are in close enough contact with people to be dangerous.

You are enjoying a great picnic. Just as you get ready to take a bite of fried chicken, you hear a high-pitched, whining sound. You are hearing the rapid beating of mosquito wings. Ouch! A mosquito has pierced your skin and is sucking your blood with its needlelike mouth.

Did you know that only female mosquitoes suck blood? Did you also know that mosquitoes spread diseases that are said to have caused half of all the deaths in human history. Let's find out more about mosquitoes.

Mosquitoes are insects. They are part of the same group of insects as flies (the Diptera group). Some of

the species of insects in this division are helpful to people, but mosquitoes are not. The 2000 known species of mosquitoes range from being a nuisance to being killers that spread diseases such as malaria and yellow fever.

These insects are usually found near water. The adults are sometimes found away from water, but the females must have water in which to lay their eggs. Young mosquitoes develop in water, too. Their habitats include rock pools, holes in trees, snow melts, rain pools, swamps, and even buckets and cans left lying about in the yard.

Both male and female mosquitoes feed on plant nectar, which gives

These mosquitoes are laying their eggs in the South American country of Ecuador. Mosquitoes lay their eggs in water.

them energy. But female mosquitoes need more than energy—they need protein in order to develop their eggs. They get this protein from blood. Just like fleas, mosquitoes are parasites, feeding on people and animals. Certain types of mosquitoes feed on their own specific hosts. For example, there is a species that feeds mainly on birds and a species that feeds mainly on people. Some species of mosquitoes can develop their first batch of eggs without a meal of blood, but these types of mosquitoes need blood for future eggs. Other types need blood to keep their eggs growing.

Blood-sucking female mosquitoes can spread diseases, especially malaria. The World Health Organization estimates that every ten seconds, someone in the world dies from malaria. There are many more people who develop malaria, but recover from it. Malaria is actually caused by another tiny parasite. When a mosquito feeds on an infected host, this parasite eventually comes to live in a mosquito's salivary glands. When a mosquito bites another host, it injects saliva—and the malaria parasite—into the new host, infecting it with the malaria parasite, too. Malaria no longer develops in the United States, but it is still present in other parts of the world.

An ancient Roman poet wrote a tale about a herdsman whose life was saved by a mosquito. The man was about to be bitten by a poisonous snake when he was wakened by a mosquito. But even this herdsman had no love for the mosquito, since he killed it along with the snake.

Like the herdsman, few of us find mosquitoes lovable. They may prove to be more useful in the balance of nature than we realize, but for now, we can at least be grateful that mosquitoes have their predators, too—dragonflies and a fish known as the mosquito fish.

Is the person that this mosquito is feeding on in danger of anything besides an itchy bump? Of the 2000 or so known species of mosquitoes, close to 100 can carry the malaria parasites that infect people.

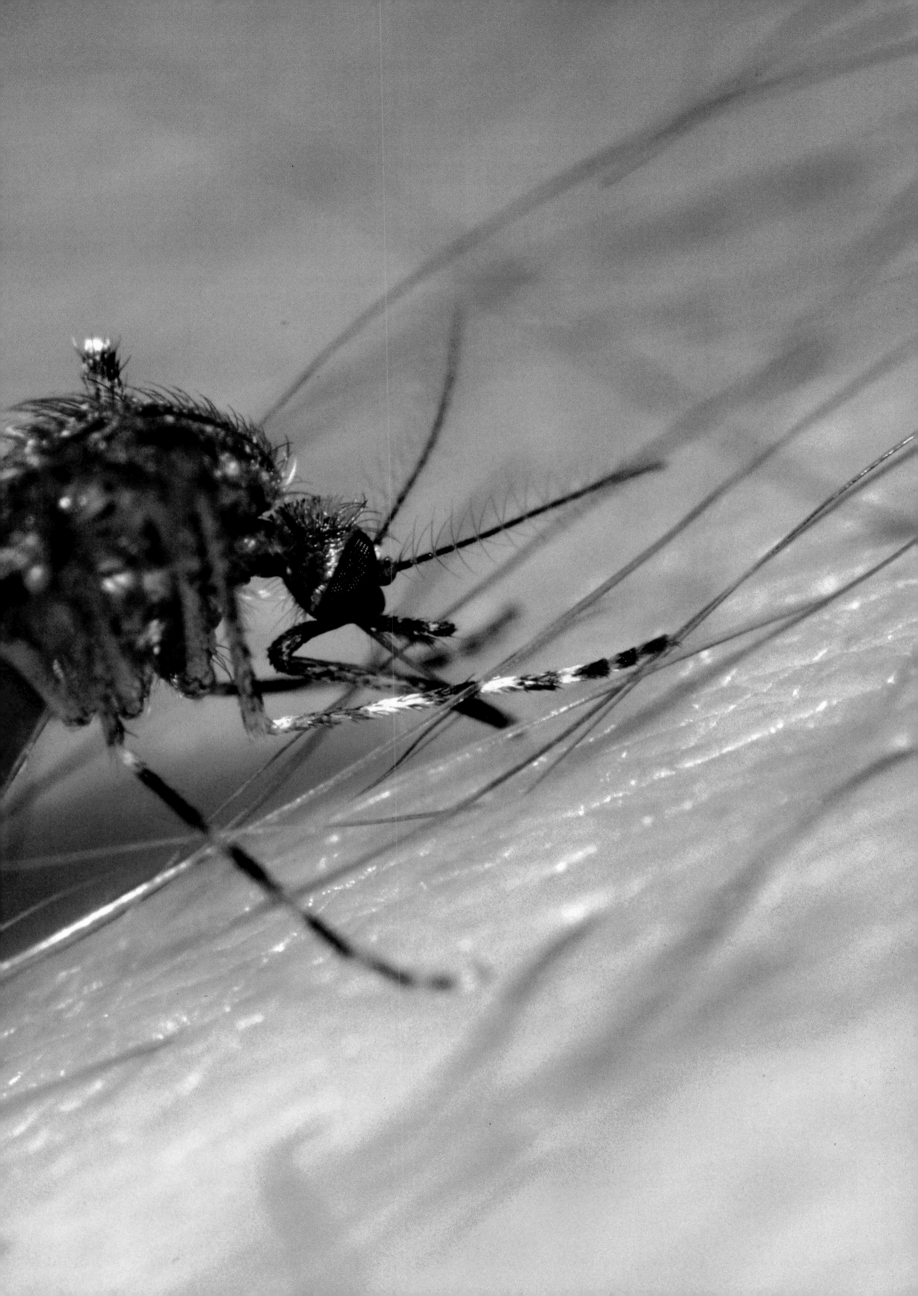

FLIES

The housefly is a common visitor in many homes. Flies can be both harmful and helpful to plants.

If you want to know how it feels to be mad enough to murder someone, lie in an otherwise quiet room in which a fly is buzzing. Buzzing and buzzing and buzzing—until you get up and swat!

Flies, like mosquitoes, are part of the Diptera group of insects. There are about 85,000 species of insects in this group. Among these are several biological families of insects, including those we call common flies. Many of the species within these families are harmful to people. The North American black fly bites livestock. A large swarm of these flies can actually kill livestock by inducing shock. Female horseflies and deer flies (the males do not feed on blood) can also cause painful bites. Flies can harm plants by spreading bacterial diseases. The larva, or young, of the Hessian fly bites wheat plants and sucks the juices—ruining the stalks.

Flies can also spread disease among people. Flies called tsetse flies are bloodsuckers. They spread a usually fatal disease called African sleeping sickness. Tsetse flies can also spread a similar disease among horses, camels, dogs, mules, cattle, and sheep. Even common houseflies, which do not bite, can spread the bacteria stuck to their feet just by walking around your house.

Believe it or not, some flies are helpful. Hover fly larvae prey on

This black horsefly belongs to one of the more than 85,000 types
of flies in the world.

plant pests known as aphids. Other flies help people by attacking harmful insects, such as corn borers and gypsy moths. Certain types of flies that infest wounded animals are also useful. They feed on the decaying tissue of the wound, leaving the healthy tissue alone. These flies also inject the wound with chemicals that help keep it from getting infected.

Flies that feed on dead animals may seem revolting, but they are helping to keep nature clean by getting rid of decaying flesh. Also, the sooner the dead animal is broken down, the sooner the minerals and chemicals in its body can be recycled back into nature.

People have found some interesting uses for flies. The African nkhungu fly is a nonbiting fly that is found in great numbers when it mates. There are so many nkhungu flies at these times that they look like a big cloud. *Nkhungu* is an African word meaning "cloud." People gather these flies in baskets, press them into cakes, dry them, and eat them! Like most insects, flies are much richer in protein than beef is.

The fruit fly, which is a pest that destroys fruit, also has its useful functions. Scientists have found that these flies are very helpful in genetic research—the study of how and why certain traits are inherited from one generation to the next.

Flies may be our enemies, but they can also be our friends. The ancient Egyptians were not wrong when they considered flies to be symbols of good luck.

Deer flies bite mammals, including humans, and suck their blood. Although deer flies are harmful, doctors can use the maggots (babies) of certain other species of flies to speed the healing of such problems as burns and ulcers.

COCKROACHES

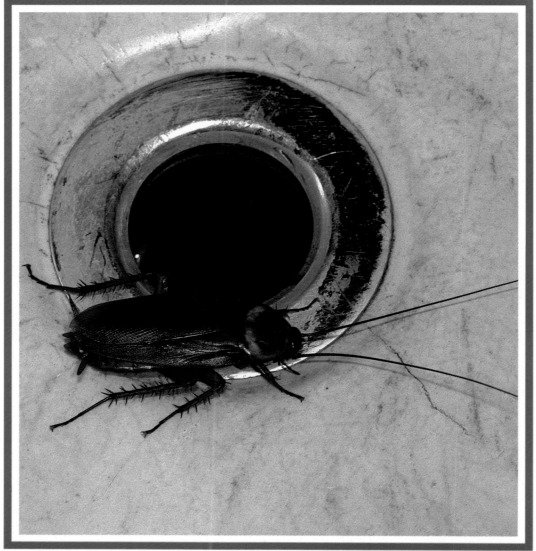

You might find an American cockroach like this one in your kitchen or bathroom sink.

If you get up for a midnight snack, you might see what scientists have called a "living fossil" running across your floor. But you will be more likely to reach for a shoe than for a magnifying glass, because this living fossil is a cockroach.

Cockroaches are insects that are also close cousins to praying mantises. There are 3500 known species of cockroaches.

Fossils of cockroaches that date back at least 300 million years have been found. Amazingly, these ancient cockroach species appear little different from modern cockroaches.

These insects like warm places, with most wild cockroaches living in the tropics. There, they live in decaying leaves, bark, and rotting wood—coming out at night to scavenge on dead insects and fallen fruit. Some species even eat wood. Most cockroaches have a brown coloring that serves as camouflage. Some species living around growing plants have patterns of yellow or green. Tropical cockroaches can be as large as 3 inches long. Some of these species fly at night.

Certain species of cockroaches have gotten used to living indoors. Their flattened bodies and wings help them to slip through cracks of buildings where they find warm places to live and free food. Cockroaches are omnivores with power-

This female roach is guarding her newborn young. Female
roaches keep their eggs safe in a hard, purselike egg case.

ful mouths for chewing. They eat every kind of food and will even eat paper, book bindings, cloth, ink, and leather. They have also been known to find free transport, stowing away with cargo being carried from place to place.

Cockroach droppings can contaminate food. Although they cannot spread diseases by sucking blood, as mosquitoes and certain flies do, cockroaches can spread germs wherever they walk. They also produce a bad smell that people find offensive.

Despite this, some scientists actually breed cockroaches. They find them useful as experimental laboratory animals. They are especially valuable to students of entomology (the study of insects).

We may find it hard to love cockroaches, but we have to admit that any animal that has lived so successfully for so long deserves our attention.

This American cockroach is snacking on a cactus flower. A roach's diet is made up of plants, food, paper, clothing, and dead insects. Cockroaches have two pairs of wings. The front pair is thick and leathery; it protects the hind wings. The hind wings are pleated and fold up like a fan.

TERMITES

Sometimes called white ants, termites are not really ants at all.

"Do you need your house inspected for termites, ma'am?"

"Certainly not! We don't have termites."

"But ma'am, I notice your porch swing has a big hole in it and the side of the house and . . ."

The termite inspector has just fallen through the porch. The lady slams the door. "Good riddance!" she says. The door, destroyed by termites, splinters into pieces.

This conversation would be a good advertisement for a termite control company, since no one wants termites destroying their home. However, termites are useful in nature. They are a good example of insects that are useful in their natural role, but whose natural function in the world causes them to compete with people.

There are about 2000 species of termites. Although a few species are found in southern Europe and over 50 species are found in the United States, most termites live in the tropics. Termites look a lot like ants and are sometimes even called white ants. Like ants and some species of bees and wasps, termites are social insects. They live in colonies with many of their own kind—each individual works for the benefit of the whole colony. In most species, these insects cannot live alone.

Anteaters can break into termite "castles," such as this one in Nigeria, and lick up termites with their sticky tongues.

A termite colony has a queen who lays eggs. She lays as many as 30,000 eggs every day. The queen keeps growing with age and can be as long as ¾ inch. She may live for 15 years or longer. The king is only ¼-inch long. He helps a queen found a colony and fertilizes her. There are other termites that can fertilize or produce eggs if the king and queen are killed or get too old to fertilize and produce eggs. There are also two types of termites in the colony that are sterile (they cannot fertilize or produce eggs). These are the workers that maintain the nest and supply food. They feed the termites that reproduce and the termites that are soldiers. The soldiers defend the nest from enemies— mainly ants.

Although they have evolved similar ways of living, termites are not closely related to ants. They are not part of the biological division that includes ants, bees, and wasps. Termites are actually more closely related to cockroaches than to ants. There are even some wild species of cockroaches that can eat and digest wood in the same way that termites do.

Termites that feed mainly on wood are able to digest it because of special bacteria and protozoa (tiny animals) that live in their digestive tracts and break down the cellulose—a component of wood. Some types of termites create termite "castles," higher than 20 feet tall, in which they live and use decaying cellulose to raise a special kind of fungi, which is their main food.

Termites are important in nature because they break down rotting trees and return nutrients to the soil to be used again. Although termites sometimes attack houses instead of trees in a forest, they are generally valuable as nature's recyclers.

While ants and bees have only female workers, this busy colony of West Coast damp-wood termites includes both male and female workers.

ANTS

Leaf-cutter ants drink plant nectar and eat insects that damage the plants.

People have mixed feelings about ants. When we buy ant farms, we admire the hard work that they do for the good of the colony.

And yet, when ants march across our picnics or set up house in our homes, we do not admire them at all! Are ants pests or are they helpful? The answer—both.

There are about 12,000 species of ants. They are found all over the world in both cold and warm areas. Ants are truly social insects. Because they live and work together in great numbers, they are more important in the world than their size would lead us to believe.

Several species are known as army ants. These are found mostly in tropical areas of India, Africa, and South America. Rather than having permanent nests, these ants travel from one area to another raiding for food. Army ant colonies are very big—they can contain from 100,000 individual ants to more than 20 million! They look like a human army on the move. Big workers with strong jaws flank the columns, scouting ahead like soldiers and leaving scent trails for the rest. The single queen is the ruler. She secretes chemicals that attract the worker ants and make them stay together.

Army ants mostly eat other insects, but when the ants are clustered in such huge numbers, they

A carpenter ant begins its recycling work by chewing holes in this piece of wood. In nature, carpenter ants are helpful.

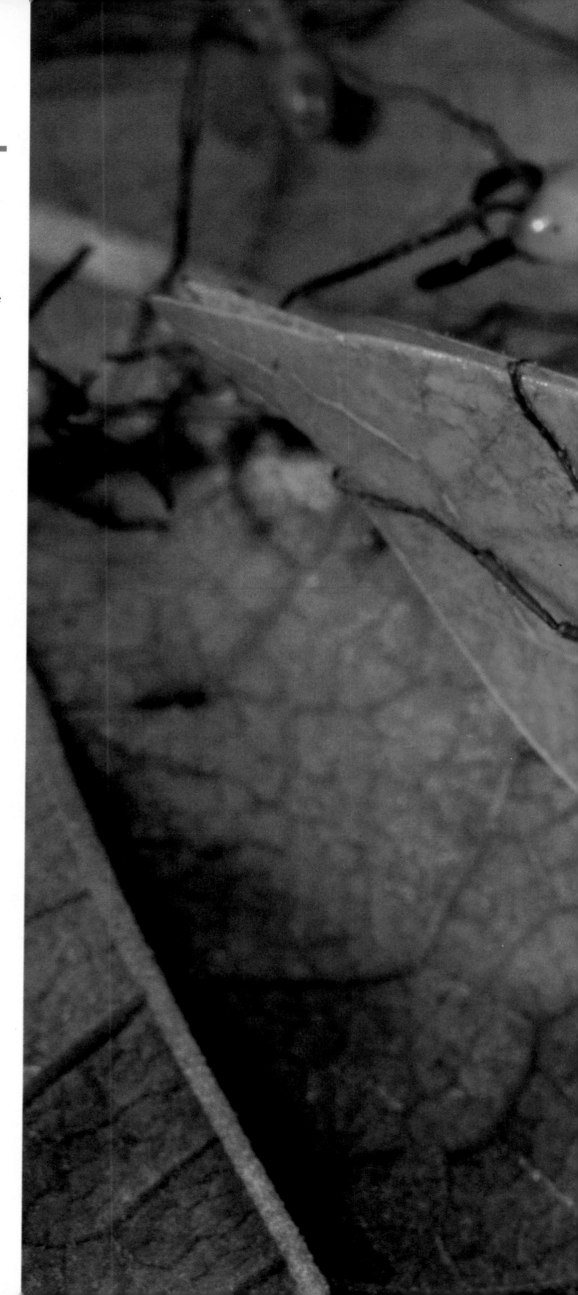

can eat animals much bigger than themselves. Lizards, snakes, even a tied-up horse is often consumed. Army ants can also march through homes in the area and bite sleeping people. But these ants can also be helpful. If people leave their houses while army ants march through, the ants will eat all of the rats, mice, cockroaches, etc., infesting their homes!

Carpenter ants are also both harmful and helpful. Unlike termites, carpenter ants do not directly feed on wood, but they do make nests in wood by chewing off pieces. If that piece of wood happens to be your windowsill, carpenter ants are harmful. If that piece of wood is a dead tree, they are helping nature recycle.

Some ants, such as leafcutter ants, cut leaves from living plants in order to grow a fungus that they eat. They cause damage when they attack plants that a farmer is trying to grow, but they enrich the soil and help the environment when they get rid of unnecessary plants.

Whether ants are considered helpful or harmful, these tiny creatures cannot be ignored. Just by sheer numbers, ants, such as army ants, can be the major predators in an area. In desert areas, they are also the major seed-eaters, affecting the populations of other seed-eating animals like rodents. Ants are also very important in spreading seeds. For example, one species gathers Trillium seeds, but eats only the outer coating, leaving the rest to grow in the new location. Ant nests and tunnels put air into the soil. Some plants are actually protected from other insects by ants. Next time you see an anthill, stop and think about these tiny and important animals before you squash them under your shoe.

These army ants are carrying away a katydid. Ants themselves are sometimes food for animals. Mountain gorillas, for example, have been filmed digging out and eating ants with great enthusiasm.

BEES & WASPS

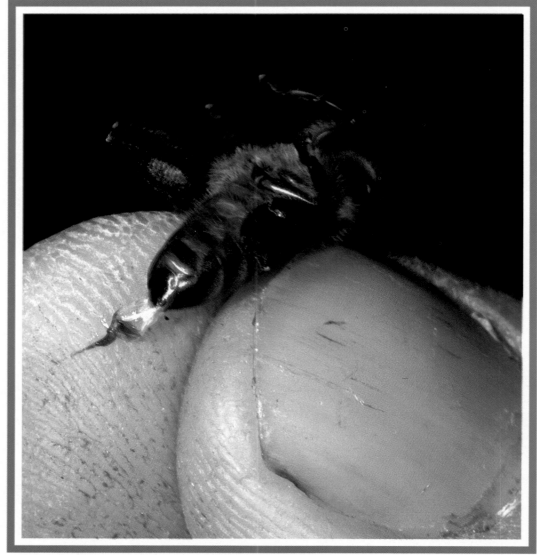

A stinging bee poses with her weapon. Only female bees and wasps have a stinger.

When people see a bee or wasp, usually their first thought is to get out of the way in order to avoid getting stung. Stings are painful, and to people with allergic reactions, they can cause death within 16 to 120 minutes. In our fear of being stung, however, we sometimes forget the good that bees and wasps do for people. The truth is that we really need these insects.

Bees, wasps, ants, and other insects belong to the same division of insects. Ants and bees are believed to have evolved from wasp ancestors.

Only females sting, since the stinger that many species of these insects has is really a modified egg-laying organ called an *ovipositor*. The ovipositor works similarly to a hypodermic needle that doctors use to give shots. Your skin is punctured with the sharp end of the hollow stinger, and the venom (or poison) that comes from a gland connected to the "needle" is pushed into the wound.

Why do many species of wasps and bees sting? First of all, not all of these insects produce venom that is dangerous to people, and second, many species rarely sting people. The original use of the stinger was for wasps to paralyze prey—usually other insects—in order to feed their young. This is still the reason why many species of wasps

The honeybee not only produces honey and beeswax, it also collects nectar and pollen.

use their stingers. Some species of wasps and bees have evolved into social insects living in a colony of many members. Each colony has a queen (or queens) that produces eggs, many workers (generally non-egg-producing females), and males (drones), whose main purpose is to fertilize the females. The males usually die after fertilizing the females. These social insects are more likely to use their stingers to protect the colony and are usually the ones that sting people.

Most bees and wasps, even those that sting, are very useful to people. You have probably enjoyed the product of one of the most social bees, the honey bee. Honey is made from the nectar that honey bees drink from plants. It is a stored energy food that the adult honey bees need to survive through the winter. Other kinds of bees and some kinds of wasps also make honey, but the honey bee is the biggest producer. Bees can survive the winter on about 50 pounds of honey. Since they can produce as much as 400 pounds in a season, the beekeeper can harvest 350 pounds.

Bees yield other useful products as well. Beeswax is used for cosmetics and candles. Even bee venom may have a use—scientists think that it may be useful for treating a joint disease called rheumatoid arthritis.

Most importantly, bees pollinate plants. (Pollen fertilizes flowers.) Pollen needs to be spread from plant to plant in order to keep plants healthy and producing fruit. Even though bees feed some of the pollen they collect to their young—pollen is very high in protein—they spread most of it from flower to flower.

Wasps are helpful, too. They prey on many insects that are harmful to crops. They are natural insect controllers.

So, while we need to watch out for the stings of wasps and bees, we should also remember that without them the world would have fewer flowers and fewer types of foods.

Yellow jackets, such as the queen and worker shown here, are also known as hornets and wasps. There are tens of thousands of wasp species in the world. In the United States, there are about 4000 species of wasps.

LEECHES

Leeches live in freshwater ponds, streams, and on land. They feed on snails, salamanders, turtles, and frogs.

"You bloodsucker!"

"You leech!"

If someone calls you a leech, you can be sure that they have insulted you. But for an animal that lives by sucking the blood of other animals, leeches can be surprisingly helpful creatures.

Leeches belong to a group of invertebrates known as annelids. *Annelid* means "ringed," and the wormlike animals in this group are generally segmented, or ringed. Earthworms, the best known annelids, are close cousins to leeches. One interesting similarity is that both leeches and earthworms are *hermaphroditic,* which means that each individual animal has both

male and female reproductive organs.

Found mostly in fresh water, leeches can also be found in the sea or on land. A few species of leeches are predators. Most species are parasites—they suck the blood of other animals.

Leeches have a sucker on their back end and a sucker on their front end. The back sucker looks like a rubber suction cup and works in much the same way. The leech attaches to an animal with its back sucker and puts its front sucker on the animal's skin, cutting it with little, sharp jaws. It has a chemical inside of its salivary glands that keeps the blood from clotting. Some

Leeches can hold blood in the side pouches of their digestive
tracts for a long time, digesting it slowly as they need it.

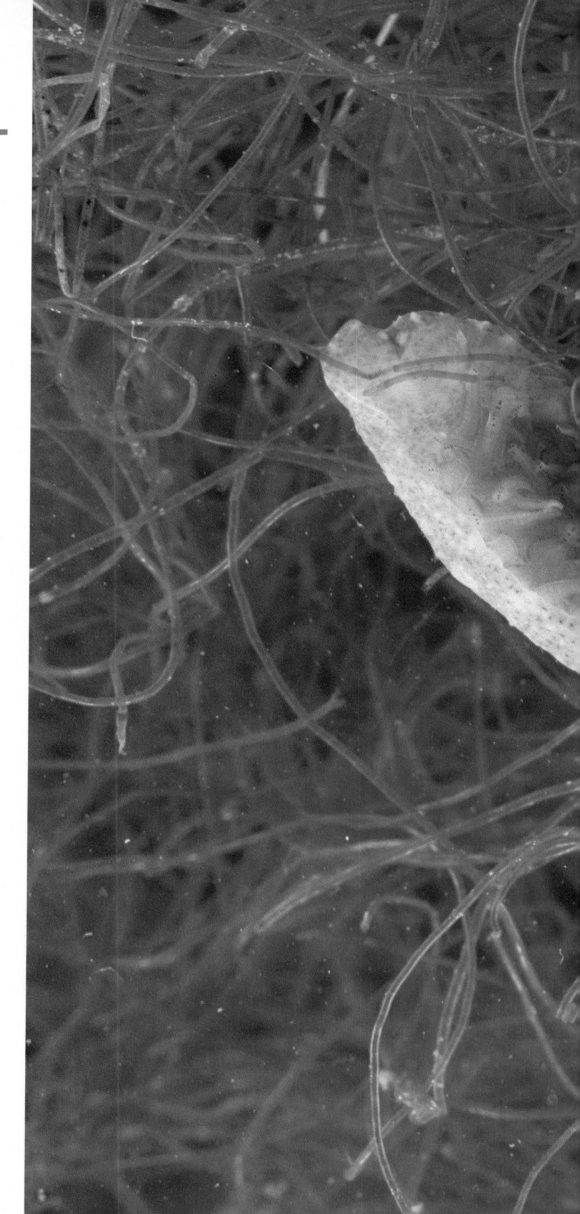

leeches also have a chemical that makes the host's blood vessels enlarge. A leech sucks blood until it is full and then drops off of the host. The chemicals that a leech secretes often cause the wounds to bleed for as long as 30 minutes after the leech drops off.

These parasites will feed on people. Plantation workers in southeast Asia suffer frequent blood loss as a result of leeches. But leeches are also helpful to people. They can be used for removing extra blood from bruises—especially black eyes. Leeches can even be bought in drugstores for this purpose.

The chemical that leeches pump into their hosts to keep blood from clotting is used as a drug for heart patients whose blood clots abnormally inside of their arteries, sometimes causing a heart attack. It is also used in certain kinds of surgery to keep blood from clotting.

Leeches can be quite pretty. Some freshwater leeches have a green back with orange spots. Leech color patterns have even been copied for designs in cloth. So the next time you see a leech, take the time to look at it closely.

This leech has its young attached to its underside. Leeches, like their earthworm cousins, are sensitive to vibrations. They also have a good sense of smell.

EARTHWORMS

This earthworm's gleaming, eyeless head is visible as it eats its way through soil.

A little girl was helping her mother plant summer flowers. Suddenly, she dropped her begonia plant and pulled back from the garden. "Oh, Mommy," she said, "there's a yucky worm." The little girl was pointing to an earthworm burrowing through the soil.

Many of us feel the same way the little girl did about earthworms. But, as her mother explained to the little girl, these creatures do have their value. The great scientist Charles Darwin said: "It may be doubted if there are any other animals that have played such an important part in the history of the world as these lowly, organized creatures."

Like leeches, earthworms are annelids (ringed, wormlike animals). They are found over much of the world, living primarily in moist soils. Most of us are familiar with medium-sized, reddish earthworms. There are also other types of earthworms, including a species that is green and one that has 600 segments. An Australian species has been measured at 11 feet long!

Earthworms must stay moist to survive. Unless they are disturbed, they only come out at night when the air is less drying. Earthworms have no eyes or ears, but they do have light-sensitive cells in their skin. They are also very sensitive to vibrations.

Earthworms are very sensitive to sunlight. If exposed to strong
rays from the sun, many species become paralyzed and die.

This cross-section of soil shows several earthworm burrows.

These annelids burrow through the soil and actually swallow soil as they make their way. Soil, which contains seeds, decaying plants, insect eggs, and small animals (alive or dead), provides the earthworms with food. The bulk of the soil passes through the earthworm and is cast around their burrows. These soil deposits are known as castings. They will also eat leaves when they are available.

Burrowing and feeding on soil make earthworms very valuable. Earthworm burrows let air enter the soil. They also allow water to drain through the soil and make it easier for plant roots to grow deeper.

Materials, such as leaves, are only partially digested by earthworms. The remains are passed out in earthworm castings and help ferti-lize the soil. Earthworms are estimated to bring up and deposit 40 tons of soil per acre in a year. The soil that passes through earthworms is excellent for growing crops—it is rich in decayed materials and it holds water better because it has been ground up in an earthworm's gizzard. As Darwin indicated, it is doubtful whether we would have enough good soil to grow food to survive without earthworms.

By bringing up soil to the surface, earthworms have also done people an unexpected service. Soil has covered and preserved ancient buildings for people to discover later.

The little girl planting begonias with her mother did not discover any ancient buildings, but she did discover that earthworms are valuable.

THE
COUSTEAU
SOCIETY

930 WEST 21st STREET   NORFOLK, VIRGINIA 23517